The MAILBOX®

The Education Center®

Prompt, Plan, Write!

Practice for **FIVE** types of writing...

- Descriptive writing
- Personal narratives
- Story writing
- Friendly letters
- Simple instructions

Written by Kim Minafo

Managing Editor: Hope Taylor Spencer

Editorial Team: Becky S. Andrews, Kimberley Bruck, Sharon Murphy, Debra Liverman, Diane Badden, Thad H. McLaurin, Jennifer Bragg, Karen A. Brudnak, Hope Rodgers, Dorothy C. McKinney

Production Team: Lori Z. Henry, Pam Crane, Rebecca Saunders, Chris Curry, Sarah Foreman, Theresa Lewis Goode, Greg D. Rieves, Eliseo De Jesus Santos II, Barry Slate, Donna K. Teal, Zane Williard, Tazmen Carlisle, Kathy Coop, Marsha Heim, Lynette Dickerson, Mark Rainey

76 Reproducible Writing Activities

www.themailbox.com

©2007 The Mailbox®
All rights reserved.
ISBN10 #1-56234-767-5 • ISBN13 #978-156234-767-3

Manufactured in the United States
10 9 8 7 6 5 4 3 2 1

Table of Contents

What's Inside

76 REPRODUCIBLE WRITING ACTIVITIES...
for independent work, center work, small-group work, and homework!

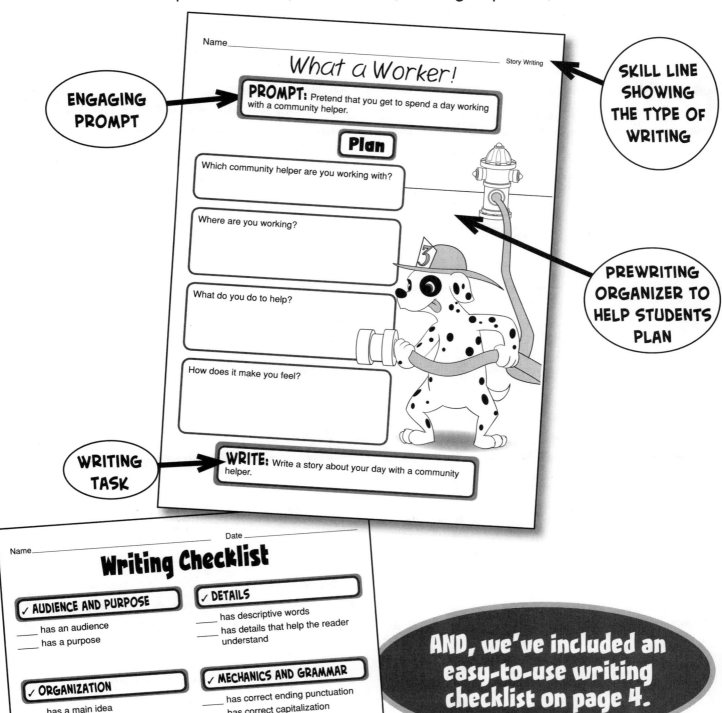

ENGAGING PROMPT

SKILL LINE SHOWING THE TYPE OF WRITING

PREWRITING ORGANIZER TO HELP STUDENTS PLAN

WRITING TASK

Name_____

Story Writing

What a Worker!

PROMPT: Pretend that you get to spend a day working with a community helper.

Plan

Which community helper are you working with?

Where are you working?

What do you do to help?

How does it make you feel?

WRITE: Write a story about your day with a community helper.

Name_____   Date_____

Writing Checklist

✓ AUDIENCE AND PURPOSE
___ has an audience
___ has a purpose

✓ ORGANIZATION
___ has a main idea
___ has details that support the main idea
___ has ideas in the correct order

✓ DETAILS
___ has descriptive words
___ has details that help the reader understand

✓ MECHANICS AND GRAMMAR
___ has correct ending punctuation
___ has correct capitalization
___ has correct spelling

AND, we've included an easy-to-use writing checklist on page 4.

Writing Checklist

✓ Audience and Purpose

_____ has an audience

_____ has a purpose

✓ Details

_____ has descriptive words

_____ has details that help the reader understand

✓ Organization

_____ has a main idea

_____ has details that support the main idea

_____ has ideas in the correct order

✓ Mechanics and Grammar

_____ has correct ending punctuation

_____ has correct capitalization

_____ has correct spelling

©The Mailbox® • *Prompt, Plan, Write!* • TEC61104

- -

Name _____   Date _____

Writing Checklist

✓ Audience and Purpose

_____ has an audience

_____ has a purpose

✓ Details

_____ has descriptive words

_____ has details that help the reader understand

✓ Organization

_____ has a main idea

_____ has details that support the main idea

_____ has ideas in the correct order

✓ Mechanics and Grammar

_____ has correct ending punctuation

_____ has correct capitalization

_____ has correct spelling

©The Mailbox® • *Prompt, Plan, Write!* • TEC61104

Braving the Bridge

Prompt: Pretend that you are walking across a bridge when you hear a troll calling out to you.

Plan

What stories have you heard about a troll and a bridge?

What does a troll look like?

How does a troll act?

What do you think a troll would want from you?

What would be a good way to answer the troll?

Write: Write a story about meeting a troll.

A Trip for Two

Prompt: You and a friend get to explore outer space in a supercharged spaceship!

Plan

Which friend will go with you?

What will you wear?

What will you see while you're in space?

What will you do while you're in space?

Where will you go?

Write: Write a story about your trip in space.

A Super Citizen

Prompt: A comic-book company asks you to invent a new superhero!

Plan

What is the superhero's name?

What is the superhero's power?

What else can the superhero do well?

What is hard for the superhero to handle?

What is the name of the superhero's enemy?

Write: Write a story about a problem the superhero has with his or her enemy. Have the story take place in your city or town.

Riding the Waves

Prompt: You are at the beach when a dolphin swims over to you. It takes you for a ride through the ocean.

Plan

Tell what time of day this happens.

Tell about the other animals you see in the ocean.	Tell about the plants you see in the ocean.

Tell where the dolphin takes you.

Write: Write about a day when you go for a ride with a dolphin.

How Old Is She?

Prompt: It's the tooth fairy's birthday. You want to throw a party.

Plan

Where will the party take place?

When will it take place?

Whom will you invite?

What do you need to buy or make?

What will you and your guests do for fun?

Write: Write a story about throwing a birthday party for the tooth fairy.

Store Surprise

Prompt: Imagine that you see your teacher at the store.

Tell the name of the store you are in when you see your teacher.

Tell what your teacher is doing when you see her.

Plan

Tell what your teacher is wearing.

Tell what is in your teacher's shopping cart.

Write: Write a story about seeing your teacher at the store.

Name_____

What a Worker!

Prompt: Pretend that you get to spend a day working with a community helper.

Plan

Which community helper are you working with?

Where are you working?

What do you do to help?

How does it make you feel?

Write: Write a story about your day with a community helper.

Say What?

Prompt: A little bird tells you a secret.

What is the bird like?

What does the bird tell you?

When does this happen?

Where are you when this happens?

What do you do after the bird tells you the secret?

Write: Write a story about a little bird telling you a secret. Give details that will make the story interesting.

A Star's Visit

Prompt: Your favorite celebrity is waiting outside your classroom door.

Plan

Who is your favorite celebrity?

Why is this person at your school?

What will happen?

When will this person leave?

Where will this person go next?

Write: Write a story about a visit from your favorite celebrity.

A "Vine" Time

Prompt: While playing outside one day, you find what looks like a rope. But soon you learn that it is a magic vine.

What do you think will happen if you climb the magic vine?

Plan

Will the vine always be magic? Why or why not?

Will you tell anyone about the vine? Why or why not?

Write: Write a story about finding a magic vine.

Lights Out

Prompt: A sudden storm knocks out the power at your school.

Plan

What are you doing when the power goes out?

How do things look or sound after the power goes out?

How do you feel?

How do your teacher and classmates react?

How do you feel when the power comes back on?

Write: Write a story about a day when the power goes out at school.

Money for the Mall

Prompt: You have won a cash prize from a local mall!
You have one afternoon to spend your prize money.

Plan

How much money did you win?

Will anyone help you spend it?

Which stores will you shop in?

What will you buy?

Write: Write a story about your mall shopping spree.

MOVING UP

Prompt: Your family will soon be moving. Where will you live? In a lighthouse!

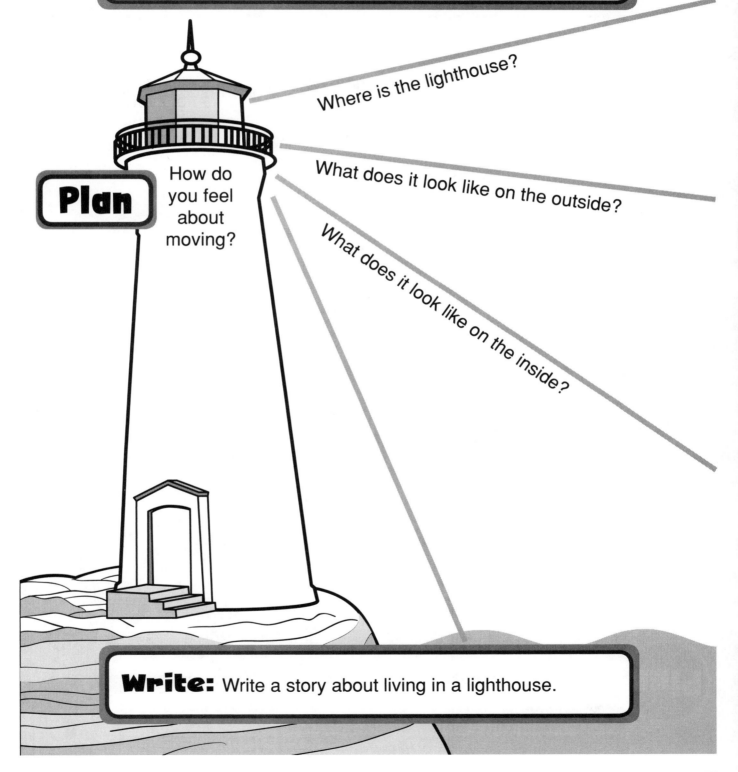

Where is the lighthouse?

What does it look like on the outside?

What does it look like on the inside?

Plan

How do you feel about moving?

Write: Write a story about living in a lighthouse.

Big Fun

Prompt: Imagine that you are a giant. Think about some of the things that are easier to do because you are so tall.

Plan

Tell about one thing that is easier to do.

Tell about another thing that is easier to do.

Tell about a third thing that is easier to do.

ONE TON
GERBIL CHOW

Write: Write a story about being a giant. Include details about the things that are easier for you to do.

Set Sail

Prompt: You have a problem while you are on a boat ride.

Beginning
Who is with you?

Where and when does the problem take place?

What is the problem?

Middle
How do you and the people with you try to solve the problem?

End
How is the problem solved?

Write: Write a story about your boat ride.

A New Plan

Prompt: You and your friends want to play basketball. But the basketball is nowhere around.

Plan

Beginning

| Which friends do you want to play with? | Where and when do you want to play? | What is the problem? |

Middle

How will you and your friends try to solve the problem?

End

How will the problem be solved?

Write: Write a story about playing basketball without the ball.

Smooth Talker

Prompt: Imagine that you have found a seashell. When you put it up to your ear, it talks to you!

Beginning

What kind of shell did you find?

Plan

When and where did you find it?

Middle

What does it tell you?

End

What will you do with the shell?

Write: Write a story about finding a talking shell.

On Your Mark...

Prompt: You enter a hopping contest against a rabbit. What happens?

Plan

First,

Next,

Then,

After that,

Finally,

Finish

Write: Write a story about your contest with a rabbit. Tell the story events from beginning to end.

Getting There

Prompt: Your parent is driving you to a friend's house but makes a wrong turn.

Plan

What happens after the wrong turn is made?

What happens next?

Then what happens?

Write: Write a story about getting lost on the way to a friend's house.

Hair-Raising

Prompt: You are walking through town. You pass a new beauty salon and look inside. You are shocked by who you see sitting in a chair.

Plan

Whom do you see?

What happens first?

What happens next?

What happens after that?

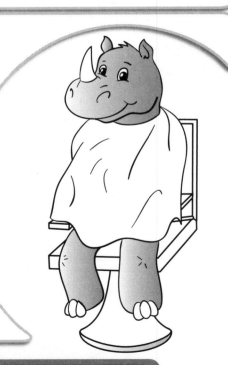

What is the last thing that happens?

Write: Write a story about the surprise you got when you looked inside the beauty salon.

Creepy Crawler

Prompt: Uh-oh! Your least favorite animal is coming toward you!

Plan

Which animal do you see?	What does it look like?	What does it sound like?
How do you feel as you watch it move toward you?		What happens next?

Write: Write a story about what happens after you see the animal coming toward you.

Missing!

Prompt: Pretend that your pet is missing.

Lost Pet

Pet's name: _____

Tell what the pet looks like.	Tell what the pet sounds like.
Tell what the pet feels like.	**Tell what the pet smells like.**

Write: Write a story about the day when your pet went missing. Describe the pet and tell what you did to find it.

Yikes!

Prompt: Think about a time when you were scared.

Plan

What happened to scare you?

How did you feel?

What did your body do when you were scared?

How did you stop feeling scared?

Write: Write about the time when you were scared.

Touch the Sky

Prompt: Think about a time when you were high in the air.

Plan

Where were you?

What were you doing?

How did it feel?

Why and how did you finally come down?

Write: Write about a time when you were high in the air. Describe what you were doing and how you felt.

The Best Ever!

Prompt: Parties take place at home, school, and friends' houses. Think about the best party you've been to.

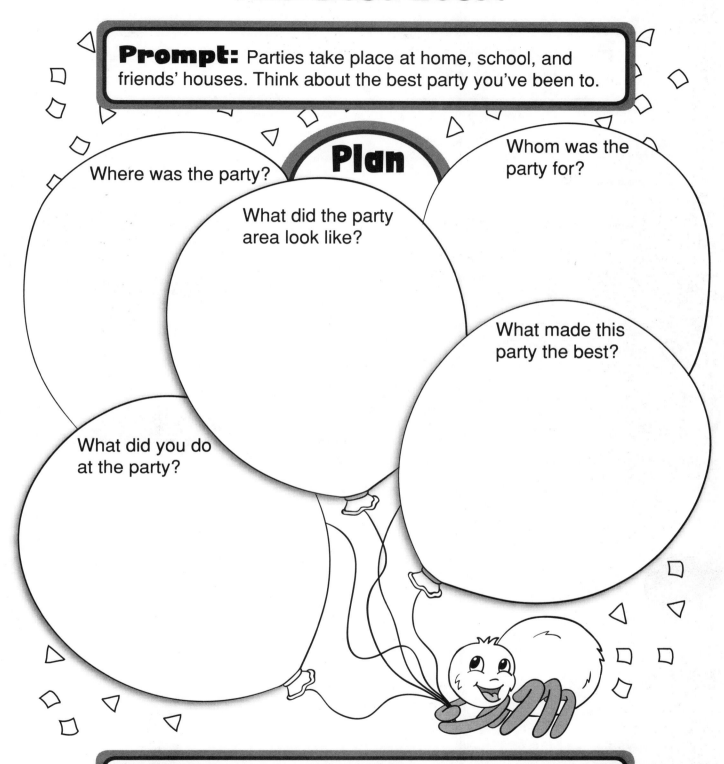

Plan

Where was the party?

What did the party area look like?

Whom was the party for?

What made this party the best?

What did you do at the party?

Write: Write about the best party you've been to. Start by telling about the place where the party was held and what it looked like. Then tell what happened at the party.

What a Ride!

Prompt: What is the most unusual thing you have ever ridden on or in?

When did you go on this ride?

What did you ride on or in?

Who was riding with you?

Plan

Where did you go?

Why do you remember this ride?

Write: Tell about the ride you took. Begin your story with a sentence that makes the reader want to read more!

Ouch!

Prompt: Think about the last time you wore a bandage.

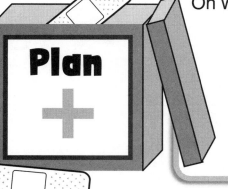

On what body part did you wear it?

When did you get hurt? Where were you?

How did you get hurt?

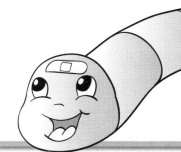

Write: Write about the time that you needed a bandage.

Shhh...

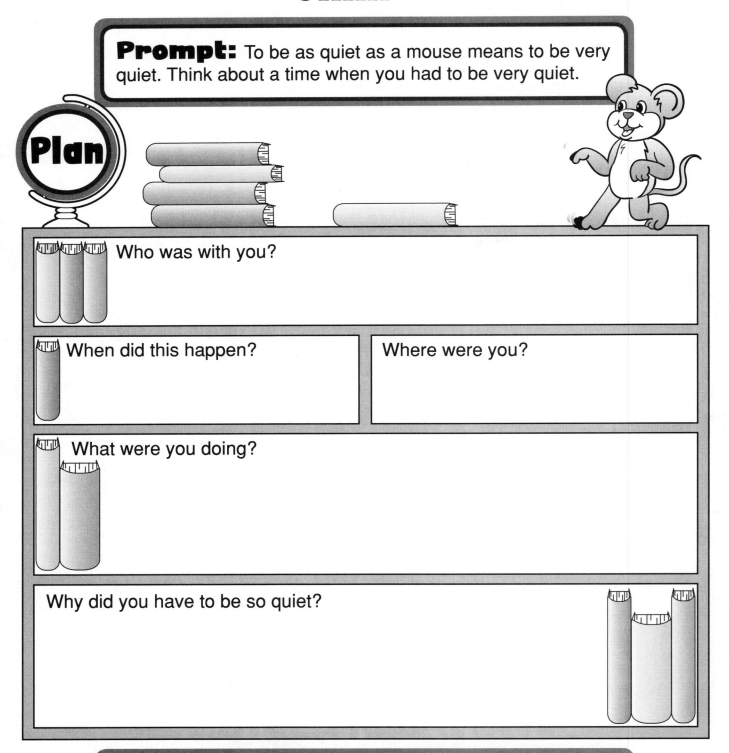

Prompt: To be as quiet as a mouse means to be very quiet. Think about a time when you had to be very quiet.

Plan

Who was with you?

When did this happen?

Where were you?

What were you doing?

Why did you have to be so quiet?

Write: Write about a time when you were as quiet as a mouse. Describe what was going on and why you had to be so quiet.

Ants in Your Pants

Prompt: When was the last time you were so excited that you couldn't sit still?

Plan

Where were you?

Who was with you?

Why were you so excited?

What happened next?

Write: Write about a time when you were very excited. Use words and details that will help your classmates understand how you felt.

Patch Up a Problem

Prompt: Think of a time when you had a problem with a friend.

Plan

How did the problem start?

How did you feel while you and your friend were having the problem?

How did you try to fix the problem?

How do you feel about the problem now?

Write: Write about the problem you had with your friend and whether it was fixed.

Miss You

Prompt: Think about a time you were away from a family member. Think about how much you missed this person.

Plan

Whom did you miss?

Where were you? Where was the person you missed?

Why did you miss this person so much?

What did you do to make yourself feel better?

Write: Write about a time when you missed a family member.

Not So Good

Prompt: Sometimes people have to eat things that they just don't like. Think about a food that you had to eat but did not like.

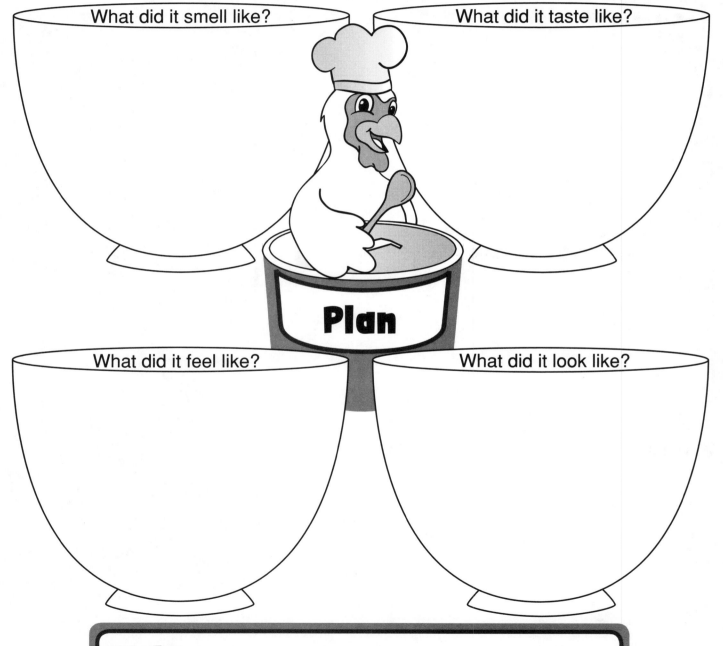

What did it smell like?

What did it taste like?

Plan

What did it feel like?

What did it look like?

Write: Write about your memory of this food. Use details to help the reader understand why you did not like it.

Are We There Yet?

Prompt: Think about a trip to or from school that took longer than normal.

Plan

Were you going to school or coming home?

How did you travel (in a bus, in a car, on a bike, by walking)?

What words tell how you felt?

Why did this trip take so long?

Write: Write about a long trip to or from school.

Clean Sweep

Prompt: Cleaning up a big mess takes time. Think about the last time you had a big mess to clean up.

What was the mess?

How long did you work to clean up this mess?

Plan

What is one thing you did to clean up this mess?

What other things did you have to do?

Write: Write about cleaning up a mess. Use details to show that it takes a long time to clean up a big mess.

Keyed Up for Fun

Prompt: Think about a time you had fun while riding in a car.

Plan

Who was with you?	Where were you going?	What happened that made the trip fun?

Write: Write about a fun car trip. Include details so the reader understands what made the trip fun.

Full of Pride

Prompt: What was something you did that made you proud of yourself?

Plan

Tell what you did that made you feel proud.

Tell one reason why you felt proud.

Tell what other people said about what you did.

Write: Write about a time when you felt proud of yourself.

School's Out

Prompt: Sometimes school gets cancelled at the last minute. Think about the fun things you did the last time this happened at your school.

Plan

What did you do in the morning?

What did you do in the afternoon?

What did you do in the evening?

Write: Write about the things you did on your day off.

The Perfect Present

Prompt: Think about a time when you had to get a present for someone.

Plan

For whom did you have to get a present? Why?

Describe your search for the present. What did you think about as you chose the present?

What present did you choose? How did you feel when you gave the present?

Write: Write about the time that you had to get a present for someone.

At the Zoo

Prompt: Think about a trip to the zoo.

Plan

Who went with you?

What did you see first?

Then what did you see?

What did you see next?

What was the last thing you saw?

Write: Write about your trip to the zoo. Tell about the things you saw in the order you saw them.

Sweet Dreams

Prompt: Dreams can be exciting! Some dreams are funny. Think about a dream you've had.

Plan

Where were you in the dream? Who was with you?

What happened first?

Then what happened?

What happened next?

What happened right before you woke up?

Write: Write about the dream you had.

Hobbies and Pastimes

Prompt: Some people collect baseball cards. Other people like to play music. What's your favorite hobby?

Plan

How do you get ready for your hobby?

Then what do you do?

What do you do next?

How do you clean up after you've finished with your hobby?

Write: Write about your hobby.

Fun to Eat!

Prompt: Eating away from home is fun! Think about a favorite place where your family likes to eat.

What does this place look like?

Plan

How does this place make you feel?

What sounds do you hear there?

What smells do you like best there?

What does this place serve that tastes really good?

Write: Name and describe the place where your family likes to eat. Help your reader understand why you like this place by clearly describing what you see, hear, smell, and taste.

Splish, Splash!

Prompt: It's fun to watch a rainstorm! Think about a time when you saw a storm.

Describe the way the rain looked.

 **Plan**

Describe the way the rain sounded. Tell if it was loud or quiet.

Describe the way the rain felt. Tell how it felt when you touched it or walked in it.

Describe the way the air smelled. Tell how it smelled before the storm, during the storm, and after the storm.

Write: Write about the storm. Use details that tell how the storm looked, sounded, felt, and smelled.

Whistle While You Work

Prompt: Some chores keep the inside of the house clean. Some chores keep the outside of the house tidy. Think about the chores you do to help your family.

Plan

List the chores that you do.

Write adjectives that describe how the house looks before you do your chores.

Write adjectives that describe how the house looks after you do your chores.

Circle the adverbs that tell how you do your chores.

carefully	badly
quickly	happily
slowly	sadly
well	often

Write: Write about the chores you do to help your family. Use adjectives and adverbs in your writing.

A Damp Camp

Prompt: Imagine that you are camping. It has been raining the entire time and you can't leave your tent.

Plan

What does it feel like to be wet?

What do you do to pass the time when it's raining?

How does it feel when you can't do what you planned to do?

Write: Write about spending a weekend in a tent while it's raining outside.

Cave Dweller

Prompt: While on a hike, you come across a cave. There's something alive inside!

Plan

Describe its size.

Describe its color.

Describe its skin.

What is it doing?

What kind of mood is it in?

Write: Write about what you saw inside the cave.

Faraway Field Trip

Prompt: Your class is taking a field trip to a school on another planet.

Plan

☆ Name the planet you are on.

☆ Tell what a classroom looks like.

☆ Tell what the students look like.

☆ Tell what the students are doing.

☆ Tell what the teacher is like.

Write: Write a report about your field trip.

Twice As Nice

Prompt: Who is the nicest person you know?

Plan

Main Idea
What is the person's name?

Supporting Detail
What is one nice thing this person does or says?

Supporting Detail
What is another nice thing this person does or says?

Supporting Detail
What is one more nice thing this person does or says?

Write: Write about the nicest person you know. Use details from your plan to support your main idea.

Looking Back

Prompt: Think about good things that have happened to you. What is the best day you remember?

Plan

What happened?

When did it happen?

Where were you?

Who else was there?

What made your best day special?

How would you feel if you had another day like this one?

Write: Write a diary entry telling all about your best day.

Book Talk

Prompt: Your teacher has asked you to tell about the events of your favorite book.

Plan

What is the title of your favorite book?

What happens at the beginning?

What happens in the middle?

What happens at the end?

Write: Plan what you will say by writing a speech about your favorite book. Be sure to include what happened at the beginning, in the middle, and at the end.

Wild Weather

Prompt: Imagine that there was a storm last night.

Plan

What kind of storm was it?

What did you see first?	What did you see after that?

Then what did you see?	How did the storm end?

Write: Write an article for a newspaper. Tell what you saw during the storm from start to finish.

A Whale of a Tale

Prompt: Oh boy! You see a huge animal!

Plan

What animal do you see?

What do you notice first about this animal?

Then what do you see?

After that, what do you see?

What is the last thing you notice about the animal?

Write: Write about the animal you see.

©The Mailbox® • *Prompt, Plan, Write!* • TEC61104

Cool Creations

Prompt: Congratulations! You've been chosen to invent a new ice cream flavor!

Plan

What does it look like?

What does it taste like?

What does it smell like?

What do you hear when you eat it?

How does it feel in your mouth?

Write: Write a description that will convince a friend to try your new ice-cream flavor.

What's Cooking?

Prompt: It's time to eat. Imagine that you go to the kitchen and find that you are having your favorite meal.

What do you see?

What do you hear?

What do you smell?

What do you taste?

Plan

What do you feel?

Write: Write a journal entry telling about your dinner.

A Change of Scenery

Prompt: Imagine that you will visit your favorite place on your next break from school.

Plan

Tell where you will go.

Tell what sights you will see.

Tell what sounds you will hear.

Tell what smells you will smell.

Tell how you will feel when you get there.

Write: Write about your favorite place. Use details that will make a reader want to go there too.

Fun for All

Prompt: Hooray! You have been chosen to help design a new piece of playground equipment.

Plan

List words that tell about the size of the equipment.

List the colors it will be.

List words that tell about the parts it will have.

List activities a child can do with the equipment.

Write: Write to your classmates about this new piece of playground equipment.

Make Your Own Cake

Prompt: If you could plan your birthday cake, what would it be like?

Plan

Tell how big or small the cake would be.

Tell the colors you would want.

Tell the designs you would want.

Tell how the cake would smell.

Tell how the cake would taste.

Tell how you would feel when you saw it.

Write: Write a paragraph that uses adjectives to describe your perfect birthday cake.

Top Choice

Prompt: You've been chosen for a big job! You get to hire a new teacher!

Would the perfect teacher be a man or a woman?

What would the perfect teacher like to teach?

What words tell how the perfect teacher would look?

What words tell how the perfect teacher would act?

Plan

Write: Write about the perfect teacher.

Writing to Red

Prompt: You have become friends with Little Red Riding Hood. Think about what you like about her.

Plan

How does she show that she is smart?

How does she show that she is brave?

How does she show that she is a friend?

How does she show that she is kind?

Write: Write a letter to Little Red Riding Hood. Tell why you like being her friend.

Field of Fun

Prompt: You and a friend are in an empty ball field. Soon, some animals come to the field and start a game!

Plan

15:00

What animals do you see?

What game do they play?

How does the game start?

What happens during the middle of the game?

How does the game end?

Write: Write a letter to your friend telling him or her about the exciting game. Be sure to tell the events from beginning to end.

Wish You Were Here

Prompt: It's time for your favorite holiday party. Your whole family will be there except for one person.

Plan

What is your favorite holiday?

What will your family do at the beginning of the party?	What will your family do in the middle of the party?	What will your family do at the end of the party?

Write: Write a letter to the family member who will not be at the party. Tell this person that you will miss him or her. Then describe the plans for the holiday party.

Out of the Pages

Prompt: Imagine that your favorite book character has come to life. Think about what you would do if you could spend a day together.

Plan

Write the name of your favorite book character.

Describe how you and the book character would start your day together.

Describe what you and the book character would do in the middle of the day.

Describe what you and the book character would do at the end of the day.

Write: Write a letter inviting your favorite book character to spend the day with you. Tell the character what you plan to do during the visit.

Lost and Found

Prompt: Oh no! Imagine you lost your favorite toy and now you have to look everywhere for it.

Plan

What did you lose?

Where will you look first?

Where will you look after that?

Then where will you look?

Where will you finally find your toy?

Write: Write a letter to a friend. Tell your friend about looking for your toy.

Dear Teacher

Prompt: Your teacher was out sick yesterday. What were some of the things you did at school while your teacher was absent?

Plan

How did your school day start?

What happened after that?

What happened in the middle of the day?

How did your school day end?

Write: Write a letter to your teacher about your day.

The Top Story

Prompt: Your class will be on the news! Think about something fun or exciting that has happened in your class this year.

Plan

What was the event?

What happened first?

What happened next?

Then what happened?

How did the event end?

CHANNEL 2 NEWS

Write: Write a letter to a TV newscaster about the exciting class event. Tell about it from start to finish.

Moon Mail

Prompt: The president has given you a big honor. You are the first kid to explore the moon.

Plan

What do you see on the moon?

What do you see when you look into space?

How do you feel when you move around?

How do you feel?

Write: Write a letter to the president. Tell him what it's like to be on the moon. Also tell him how it feels to be the first kid to explore it.

A Lucky Day

Prompt: You travel to the end of a rainbow. When you get there, you find a pot of gold!

Plan

How long do you travel before you find the gold?

What does the gold look like?

What is near the gold when you find it?

What does the pot look like?

Write: Write a letter to a leprechaun. Describe finding his pot of gold.

Change of Address

Prompt: Pretend that you are a puppy from the pet store. You have just been taken home by a family.

Plan

Where do you live?

What is your new home like?

Whom do you live with?

What is the best thing about your new home?

Write: Write a letter to one of your brothers or sisters. Tell him or her all about your new home and new family.

Fishy Feeding

Prompt: Imagine that you are going on vacation. You must leave directions for a friend so she or he can feed your pet goldfish while you're away.

How many times a day does your fish need to be fed? When?

What kind of food does your fish eat? How much?

Plan

Where do you keep the food?

What should be done after the fish eats?

Write: Write directions that tell how to feed the goldfish. Make sure you include everything your friend needs to know.

Caterpillar Coach

Prompt: A lot happens when a caterpillar changes into a butterfly. Imagine that you have been asked to explain each step to a caterpillar.

Plan

What will happen to the caterpillar first?

Then what will happen to it?

What is the last thing that will happen to the caterpillar?

What will happen next?

Write: Explain the changes in the order in which the caterpillar can expect them.

What Time Is It?

Prompt: Your friend can only tell time on a digital clock. He wants you to teach him how to tell time on a clock with hands.

Plan

What will you teach him first?

Then what will you teach him?

What will you teach him next?

What's the last thing you will tell him?

Write: Write a set of instructions that will help your friend learn how to tell time.

Cool Tips

Prompt: It's snowing! Your neighbor wants to build a snowman, but she's never built one before. You decide to teach her how to build one.

Plan

What's the first step?

What's the second step?

What's the third step?

What's the last step?

Write: Write your neighbor instructions for building a snowman.

Number, Please

Prompt: You've been asked to teach a younger child how to make a phone call.

Plan

What should the child do first?

What should the child do next?

Then what should the child do?

What is the last thing the child should do?

Write: Write instructions for how to make a phone call. Make sure your instructions are in order.

Fire Drill

Prompt: Imagine that your class has a substitute teacher. She needs to know what to do if the fire alarm rings.

Plan

What do students do to get ready to leave the room?

What does the teacher do?

Where does the teacher take the class?

What does the class do when the fire drill is over?

Write: Tell what the class and teacher should do if the fire alarm rings. Make sure your instructions are in order.

Fresh and Fruity

Prompt: The principal is hungry! You are asked to make a fruit salad for this important person.

Plan

List the fruits you will use.

List the steps you take to make the salad.

Now write adjectives that describe the fruit salad.

Write adjectives that describe the fruits you use.

Write: Write directions for making a fruit salad. Use lots of adjectives in your writing.

A Sweet Ending

Prompt: Your teacher wants to celebrate the end of the school year by throwing a party. She is going to let you make your own ice-cream sundae!

Plan

List the flavors of ice cream and the toppings you want to use for your sundae.

List the steps you will follow to make your sundae.

Write adjectives that tell about the sundae.

Write: Explain how you will make your sundae. Use one or more adjectives in each step.